Angie Quitas

Nata... Embra your Beat! :) Angie O

Let's Do This!

A Good Vibes Guide to Finding Your Inner Beat

Cover by Phil Studdard/Flip Design Studio

Graphic Design by Brenda Hawkes

Editorial Direction by Phyllis Jask

Acquisition Editor Anne Bruce

Front and back cover photos by Alycia Moreno, Grace Rising Media

Printed in the United States of America

ISBN: 978-1087898636

To my "gram"—you gave me my first glimpse of

what it looks like to embrace my vibe.

It's all done hunny, it's all done.

COLLECTIONS

HEY!

For a long, long time I used to think I was weird. I mean, I am weird! But SO WHAT?! I was trying to keep all my talents hidden. Why? Because they didn't look like everyone else's? They SHOULDN'T! When I embraced my beat—my vibe, my energy, my confidence, my inner vibe, my joy!—I shifted my mindset about being weird from a bad thing into a good thing. OH YEAH! Just like that...my beat became clear as day!

My thoughts, my ideas, my creativity make up my beat—and it's mine and mine alone, just like your beat is yours. I'm not worried anyone will steal my vibe, and you shouldn't worry about anyone stealing yours, either. That's the meaning of life as far as I'm concerned. We can nod along and dance with each other, but we still have our own individual vibe. And that's the best thing ever! Wouldn't the world be so boring if we were all the same?

Finding your beat is your path to embracing your energy and attitude. It's building your confidence, style, and vibe, and welcoming every bit of your inner groove with open arms and an open heart! When you shift your mindset from comparing yourself to what others think of you to loving yourself for who you are, you change your game. You can achieve your goals with an inner conviction and confidence you never knew you had. All the vibe-getting strategies I offer are free. All you have to do is put your time into implementing them.

The tips I share in this book are all connected. I use them to power through my days and fill my self-love bucket to the brim. A domino effect occurs: improved self-love leads to better attitude, which leads to boosted mood, which leads to improved energy, which leads to more confidence, which leads to healthier relationships, which leads to more smiling! **WINNING!**

How do you channel your beat to fuel your days? I feel my energy on the inside and wear it on the outside through movement and fun and funky styles. Action and wardrobe are important to me because they are my outer expressions of my inner vibe. The HYPE is real and I am responsible for creating the daily hype in my household. My attitude sets the tone for my day and for the others who I interact with. So believe the hype and just run with it!

I power my beat through my three love languages—music, dance, and energy. Music is good for the soul, and it inspires movement and energy! It can instantly change my mood and transport me to another time and place. Throughout the book, I've sprinkled some of my favorite energy-boosting playlists to inspire you to create some of your own!

It's my hope for you to channel your own beat, vibe, confidence, and energy to create a life lived with joy. I've shared the tools that work for me in the hope you can adapt them to boost your energy, happiness, and productivity! **I love life and want you to, too!**

—Angie Q

"I want my **light** and **energy** to be so **bright** you have to wear sunglasses around me."

Attitude

Channeling Your Vibe

Our vibe is our energy and part of who we are. It's the BAM! behind our actions. It's invisible but you can feel it. My hippie soul is all about good vibes and big energy. If my energy is low, it affects my day. I've found ways to keep it in the yellow—if my energy were a color it would be bright, bouncy, yellow…with a big smile! Oh! And it would be dancing! How would you describe your energy?

PLAY THAT FUNKY MUSIC

Music is one of my love languages, so of course this is part of a mood booster. When I feel *meh*, I go to my hype music and find the "Get Out of the Funk Playlist." Really, it's a regular ol' concert up in my house, but guess what? It works!

Boosting your mood with music is one of the easiest strategies you can implement. Think about it all—you are singing, so you've taken your mind off of whatever problem you had, and naturally you will want to move a little, which in turn kicks on those endorphins. I stick to a playlist with upbeat lyrics, tunes, and positive messages. Music is therapeutic and this jam session is free of charge.

Make Time for Yourself

Taking a moment to check yourself is self-love, and it's not selfish! Even if you're thinking you don't have time, make the time—even if it's 10 minutes every day. I double dog dare you to make time for yourself! You didn't think my 10-year-old-self could walk away without a double dog dare, did you?

REDISCOVER YOUR HAPPY KID ACTIVITY

I rediscovered an energy strategy that seems so simple yet I had forgotten about...the happy kid activity. I started incorporating activities I loved when I was younger. Think back to what you used to love to do when you were little, but then life got busy, you grew up, and that part of you got buried. **Come on, I got you!** Let's uncover the true you. Think back to what you used to love to do when you were 8, 10, or 12 years old. Was it biking, dancing, jump roping, skateboarding? **Do it!** You owe it to yourself!

For me it was roller skating. Little 8-year-old me could out-skate any boy on a bike, and it felt incredible! So last Christmas I asked for and received roller skates. I even felt like a little kid when I opened them up. Later that morning, 42-year-old me was outside roller skating—along with all the other 8-year-olds who were trying out their gifts—and it **FELT INCREDIBLE!** I crave skate breaks now because I know the positive effect they have on my day.

"Energy is like pixie dust. It leaves a trail as if to say, *Yes! You've been here!*"

SHARE YOUR ENERGY

I like to call this a trade-for-a-trade, like when I was a kid and I'd swap lunch snacks with my friends. Don't even think about trading me those raisins for my **Oreos** and **Cheez-Its!** Oh no! It's the same thing with your mood—don't come at me with raisins. Every time we come in contact with somebody, we share our mood and energy with each other. I always ask myself when I come in contact with someone, "Am I adding value to their life?" When you come in contact with someone, are you giving them Cheez-its and Oreos, or **dried-up raisins?**

Mood Mover Tip!

If you feel like you are not in the best mood, please do not share that with anyone else. I'm not saying don't ask for help if you need a boost, but try not to be a downer and drag others into your funk. Find your inner vibe to turn that around with your favorite mood booster! I call this my "check yourself moment." You can get it together! And if you're really struggling, reach out to a trusted friend or professional for help. There's no shame in asking for help!

Q the Music

Life's inevitable bad days, bad moments, and bad news happen, but what you do with that energy is your choice. Give yourself a small amount of time to **reflect** on it, **acknowledge** it sucks, and then deal with it. Then move on because you got some life to **live!** A sure fire way to get out of the funk is to blast your fave music and have a dance party of one. Movement is powerful and can flip the switch in your brain.

This is what's on my Get Out the Funk playlist.
What's on yours?

I'm Addicted to Your Light:
Beyonce

Before I Let You Go:
Beyonce

Survivor:
Destiny's Child

Calma:
Pedro Capo
(Alicia Keys remix)

Shake It Off:
Taylor Swift

Dog Days Are Over:
Florence and the Machine

Me and Bobby McGee:
Janis Joplin

What You Know:
T.I.

Can't Stop the Feeling:
Justin Timberlake

Good to Be Alive:
Andy Grammer

Follow "Angie Quitasol" on Spotify to get all my playlists.

13

WELCOME ALL ACTIVITIES

Every day we have lists of the stuff we love doing and the stuff we have to do (like laundry, **blah!**). My system is a lot like Nike's: **Just Do It.** Put your best foot forward on everything you do, even the have-to-do's. Even if you don't enjoy doing them, you'll feel the accomplishment of having knocked them off your list. Bonus: you free up time for the stuff you really want to do.

Q the Music

An energetic playlist is a guarantee to put that pep in your step as you tackle those have-to-do's, like cleaning. I can always count on two helpers to clean with me every Saturday: The Rolling Stones and Mary J. Blige.

Start Me Up:
Rolling Stones

Real Love:
Mary J. Blige

Not Gon' Cry:
Mary J. Blige

(I sing this one loud! For the record I'm happily married but this takes me back to *Waiting to Exhale* and I'm singing for every woman wronged!)

I Can Love You:
Mary J. Blige
(featuring Lil Kim)

Sweet Thing:
Mary J. Blige

Beast of Burden:
Rolling Stones

I'm Goin' Down:
Mary J. Blige
(You have to jump up on the tub and belt this out! The Windex bottle serves as your microphone!)

I Used to Love Him:
Lauryn Hill
(featuring Mary J. Blige)

Gimmie Shelter:
Rolling Stones

Sympathy for the Devil:
Rolling Stones

Miss You:
Rolling Stones

Paint It Black:
Rolling Stones

CHANGE YOUR SCENERY

If you can, take a day trip. Explore a town you've never visited, take a hike, become one with nature, **go somewhere new.** This is life giving! It will recharge your battery so you are ready to bring your A Game to your next task. If you can't get away, take an online 3-D tour of someplace you've never been.

Embrace Physical Activity and Music

Movement and music run a neck-and-neck race for best vibe-getting, energy-grabbing strategies. They are my two OG friends. Much like my kids, they constantly fight for attention but I love them both the same! Movement combined with music can instantly make you feel better.

What are the benefits? Movement **boosts** your mental health and music gets you moving! The benefits will keep you going, and you will begin to carve this into your routine. And that is when you get creative. You can walk down the stairs instead of taking the elevator, park at the farthest end of the parking lot, play catch with your kid outside, walk around the building at lunch, do jumping jacks in between Zoom calls, lunge to the mailbox and back. **Have a dance party of one!** I feel like every day deserves a 5:00 dance party! The endorphins will kick in and you will be good to go!

66 There is **power** in movement. 99

YOU'VE GOT TO MOVE IT!

Movement is proven to reduce stress, ward off anxiety, and boost self-esteem. So anytime you are feeling funky or have a low energy, get up and move! Choose any movement. Walk around the block, do some jumping jacks, skate, pushups, etc. Anytime I feel the funk come on I say, "Hey Alexa, play that funky music." And I dance! It only takes half a song and I'm back on track. Now if you need double the boost, head on outside for a lungful of fresh air and physical activity. **Oh yeah!** You will feel like a whole new person.

How can you implement this in your daily routine? Look at your life and find time in your day to incorporate movement. Some days it will be a full 30 minutes and others it will only be 3. All of this comes down to consistency.

Start It Up!

How do you start your day? On any given morning at 6:00 you will find me in our home gym working out. In between sets I'm having a full on dancing-in-the-mirror-lip-syncing concert! A concert is exactly what occurs every day in the Quitasol gym. Physical movement is essential for me, and sets an energetic tone for the rest of my day.

Q the Music

Music can make or break your workout or your mood. Have you ever forgotten to charge your AirPods and had no music for a run or a training session? <<Cue the horror music!>> It's as if you are dragging yourself through mud... it is sluggish and you don't get the **hype** you wanted for the workout. Because I like so many different types of music, my workout playlist is forever evolving. Here's one I am currently vibin' to:

Country Girl (Shake It for Me):
Luke Bryan

Feelin' Myself:
Will.i.am featuring Miley Cyrus

Work B%* &h:
Brittany Spears

Mi Gente:
Beyonce & J Balvin
(homecoming live)

I Love Rock and Roll:
Joan Jett & The Blackhearts

Forever:
Drake, Kayne, Lil Wayne, Eminem

1999:
Prince

Let's Go Crazy:
Prince

Stupid Love:
Lady Gaga

Whoomp! There It Is:
Tag Team 9
(This is the song we played when my hubby and I walked into our wedding reception. Good memory!)

Creep:
TLC

Africa:
Toto

ADJUST YOUR ATTITUDE

When you start to feel the funk—that bad mood—come on, you have bad vibes. I like to refer to attitude as a power tool because it should have a warning label that reads HANDLE WITH CARE. One moment you can be doing just fine and then the next, you're thinking, "Hey, I thought we were cool?" How do you switch your attitude?

You need an AA! That is an **attitude adjustment!** Don't come up here with all that bad energy. (Note: this is actually how I talk to myself!) Funky, tired, bad, and sad moods happen to all of us. They can hit us out of the blue or we can feel them coming on. How do we combat vibe-busting, energy-sucking, bad moods? Mood boosters come in many forms, like music, meditation, or movement— or whatever healthy thing you need to do to lift your spirits and energy.

Q the Music

Midday I always need a pick me up. This comes in the form of a 3:00 iced coffee, a skate break, and some good music. It's the modern-day entrepreneur break!

Savage Remix:
Megan Thee Stallion (featuring Beyonce)

Good as Hell:
Lizzo

Flawless Remix:
Beyonce (featuring Nicki Minaji)

Can't Nobody Hold Me Down:
Puff Daddy

Let's Get Down:
Tony! Toni! Tone!

Feel So Good:
Mase

Night Crawling:
Miley Cyrus (featuring Billy Idol)

Bennie and the Jets:
Elton John

I Can See Clearly Now:
Johnny Nash

Flashlight:
Parliament

21

Style

Energizing Your Brand

What we wear on the outside can be a reflection of how we feel on the inside. Our style is our own personal brand. Have you ever tried on a garment in your closet and it changed how you feel in that moment? (Hint: it should make you feel amazing!!) On those days when I feel off, I reach for an outfit that reflects the mood I want to have—bright, sunny, energetic, ready to take on life—and it lifts my spirits in the time it takes me to get dressed. A good look can power my day and make me feel invincible. What does your style do for you?

Embrace Your Style

Style is a big energy thing with me. My confidence and energy radiate outward through my style. Do you feel bad ass or run-down? Your outfits should make you feel as good on the outside as you do on the inside. If you feel vibrant, why hide behind a hoodie?

You have a common thread throughout your style evolution, but your style is forever shifting with your personal transformation and **growth** at different stages throughout your life: **first job, new baby, retirement, divorce, career shift,** you name it. Who you were before those pivotal moments is no longer around. That person has left the dance floor. What happened? You think to yourself, "Wow, that happened fast. **Who am I? What do I like?** *Style*? I'm trying to survive over here, I can't think about style."

I say, rock that common thread through your style evolution! You might not want to wear the same fashion from your teens when you're 50, but you could channel the same vibe into an outfit you feel comfortable in for the current stage of your life. Own your look and be the **fabulous** you you're meant to be!

My Style Evolution

As we age, we have shifts in our identity and our style reflects this change. I vividly remember my first style evolution. I had just had my second child and one soon-to-be 3 year old. It was the morning of my daughter's 3rd birthday. Oh, I have vivid thoughts of this moment! I was sitting on the floor in my closet. I can see myself right now picking away at the carpet, feeling lost and insecure. Lost! **"Who the hell am I?** Why is my sister bossing me around?" (Yes, my sister is in the closet with me.)

As she grabbed garments off the hanger and threw them into a pile, she proceeded to show me some serious tough love: **"This is out of style!** You'll never wear this again! You need accessories. Ang, **What the heck is *this*?"**

My closet—like my ego—was stripped down to a couple of lonely garments and denim that was squeezing my C-section shelf. This was a pivotal moment for me, and I embraced the stage I was at in my life. We all will have these moments: **How do I find myself?** I looked at my nearly empty closet and saw a clean slate!

CHANNEL YOUR CONFIDENCE THROUGH STYLE

What you wear is an expression of who you are. Your own personal style is part of your confidence and voice. So in your everyday moments, you should go back to basics. My number one rule in style confidence is this: **If you like it wear it!**

Don't worry what others will think! Your voice should come through your look. It's a reflection of **"you"—the glorious you!** Only wear garments that make you feel alive. Yes, we all have that outfit that makes us feel like the baddest B out there. The day you wear that look, you are kicking ass and taking names.

❝ Your outfit is the base of everything in your day. It's more than clothes; it's a persona, an attitude, a vibe! ❞

You gotta start where you are and with what you have already! Here's how to do a style inventory.

1 Assess Your Style

Get a notebook or open up notes in your phone...we are going to go to **signature style** school! You owe this to yourself! Look in your closet. Do you have garments that make you feel like the baddest B? If so, take a moment and really look at those garments. What do they have in common that make you feel so damn good? Is it the color? The print? The cut? The style? Start making a list of the clothes that make you **feel alive.** This is your list; no one else is going to see it, so be free and have fun with your choices.

Mine looks like this: faux leather anything, bodysuits, big earrings, bright heels, flares. What are yours?

2 Go Digital

Open Pinterest and create a private, **signature style board** and start

pinning all the looks that speak to you! If you noticed you love a printed dress, search "printed dresses." Your signature style board will help you when shopping for new looks and it will help you edit your current closet situation.

3 Edit Your Closet

This one might hurt. If it no longer serves or represents the glorious you, **Get rid of it!** It's only causing chaos in your life. Every time you put on a garment ask yourself, "Does this represent my authentic self?" I follow these 3 simple rules when I edit my closet:

- **Don't force anything!** You know the pieces I'm talking about...that garment you take off your hanger but it never makes it onto your body. It never even leaves your closet. **Freeloader!** It's not you anymore, but you try to force it and think, "One day I can wear this to a girls brunch." No, you really won't!

- **Don't hesitate.** Do you hesitate when reaching for the garment? Even if it is a split second of hesitation, the garment needs to go! Hesitation in wearing that garment can mean many things: you really don't like it, you don't feel good in that garment, you bought it on a whim and it's really not your style. (Oh, that's a big one. Impulse and clearance buying is always a recipe for a dud. 100% every time. Disclaimer: I love a good deal! In no way am I saying clearance shopping is bad. Saving money is good. It's great to get a deal but if it's not your style and becomes a freeloader in your closet, it's bad.)

- **Find your "I'm the baddest B" garment.** Which garment in your closet right now is your "I am the baddest B" garment? Is it the clearance find or the random dress you bought because you needed it for a last minute event? I doubt it. The "I am the baddest B" garments in your closet are the pieces you choose intentionally. Before purchasing a garment I meet with the closet committee—me and the other tenants in my closet—and we don't let just any old sweater or dress in our territory. No! It has to make the cut and answer these questions: Is it part of my signature style? Does it make me feel alive? Do I feel like my true authentic self wearing it?

Get Rid of It If It Doesn't Fit

This one is a hard one, too. You may be telling yourself, "But, but, but I swear I will lose 5 pounds so I can wear those jeans again." Do not even put yourself through that stress and bad energy. I find that keeping garments in my closet that do not fit my current body only makes me feel bad about myself. A taunting too-tight, can't-button-denim in my closet is not my friend! In fact, those jeans represent negative self-talk, and honestly I will not allow that in my closet. **Bye-bye!**

Mood Mover Tip!

Never underestimate the power of a good outfit. It's my armor of confidence and high energy. I have three go-to mood boosting looks! They all start with **color!** Ok, **color** and **killer shoes!** That's right! Mama is taking back this day in hot pink heels. No, I didn't stutter! Heels and a faux leather pant and watch out world! Instantly my mood is on fire!

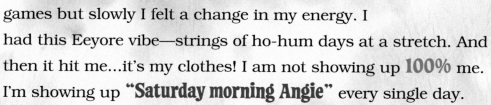

Coming out of a year of quarantine or semi self-isolation, I believe we all can attest to the power of a great outfit. Wearing loungewear, joggers, and tees can take a toll on your confidence. In the beginning it was all fun and games but slowly I felt a change in my energy. I had this Eeyore vibe—strings of ho-hum days at a stretch. And then it hit me...it's my clothes! I am not showing up **100%** me. I'm showing up **"Saturday morning Angie"** every single day.

From that point, I conducted my own very mood booster experiment. I only wore joggers and no makeup one day a week. I wanted to see if this is a me thing or is this an everybody thing. If I feel this way, I thought others must be feeling the same thing, too. So I did a style challenge with all of my clients. On Sunday I texted my clients with a style challenge for the week: "All right people, here's our style challenge for the week. Monday: color. Tuesday: stripes. Wednesday: wear your favorite topper. Thursday: fancy day.

Friday: graphic tee. (I used to do this as a teacher, too. I would have a 5th grade teacher style challenge, where we would theme the week and show up for our students.) We would share our looks via text for that day. The response was insane! I felt so much better about myself that week! I had a reason to clean up. I was more productive.

Boosting your mood is for yourself but also for the others around you. We want to spread good energy, not bad vibes. When we show up for ourselves we show up for others. You can create your own weekly challenge when planning your week on Sunday (refer to Prep Your Week on Sunday section). **You got this!!**

"It is your responsibility to take you to the next level."

Confidence

Finding Your Beat

Finding your beat is tapping into your confidence. Your energy fuels your confidence. How you energize yourself is as unique as you are! Is it having time to yourself or being around a group of people you love and admire? What gets your energy flowing? What do you need to restore yourself to yourself?

Connect with your beat...is it putting on your favorite outfit? Walking on the beach or through a forest? Connecting with friends? Listening to an amped up song? Use whatever you need in order to power you!

66The moment you **believe** you have what it takes...that is when you are **unstoppable.**99

OWN YOUR BEAT

Turn up your volume! There are so many different beats out there and that's what makes this world dynamic and interesting. Hiding your beat is essentially hiding your talents from yourself and the world.

Last year, I had a "she-shed" (called a Journee) built out of necessity. Add this up: my kids in online school from home plus my husband who loudspeaker-volume talks plus an 1,800 square foot home equals a mama who needed her own workspace! The gentlemen who built my Journee could *build*—that was his beat. He was talented, good with math (he tried to explain his plan to me in engineer-speak and I just stared at him with that lost look in my eyes), and he took my vision and made it reality. I could tell he loved doing what he does! My point is every day I am still amazed at his work. I tell my husband, "Babe, he's a **builder!** He *built* this from scratch."

Someone out there needs your expertise on building, cooking, gardening, pottery, editing, organization, etc. Your beat is worthy and so are you!

LIVE OUT LOUD

You will believe anything you tell yourself. Think about that. If you were to measure your self-talk, would it be more positive or negative? You are in control of how you treat yourself. When it comes down to presenting yourself confidently in public situations, you have to **stop worrying about what others think.** Remind yourself: **I am enough! I like me!**

It's night and day when you make this shift, and you will shine. The shift will attract others to your light. And I remind myself this all the time. Life is about adopting a learner's mindset and exposing yourself to new points of view. When you take yourself out of the equation, you open yourself to a whole new set of experiences.

> ## *Mood Mover Tip!*
>
> Don't worry about what others think. Do what makes you happy, gives you inner fulfillment, and sparks joy. Practice daily affirmations. Do not compare yourself to others. Give yourself grace to be your best you.

PRACTICE POSITIVE SELF-TALK

What you tell yourself is far more important than any other strategy. Picture this: you've had a rough day and call a friend or a family member who gives you the biggest hype talk ever. They tell you how amazing you are, list all your best qualities, and go on and on. You get off the phone and say to yourself, *"I'm still not all that."* You don't believe them!

The most important hype person is you! No one else. If you do not love yourself, you will never truly be confident in yourself. It all starts in your mind and how you talk to yourself. Feed your mind with positive self-talk. Be kind to yourself! Anytime you feel negative self-talk creep in, repeat a self-love affirmation to fight that negative thought.

APPRECIATE YOUR AGE

Appreciate your moment and be confident with your age. What you have to say and offer has no age requirement. What it really comes down to is this: Am I relevant? Am I adding value? Am I being authentic? You can be 82 and still speak of confidence, style, goals, and affirmation. **You're the boss!**

I like to surround myself with people of all different ages, especially when it comes to work because I can learn from everyone! I know that as a 42-year-old woman working in social media, I need to work with individuals who are in their 20s. Remember, the learner's mindset is where you want to live! New trends, strategies, and a zest for life is what I crave from interacting with my 20-something crew. Now, my 50-and-over crew? I want to soak in all their wisdom. I respect their experience and want to learn from them.

Age confidence thrives when you put yourself in learner territory. My list of learner activities this year? Complete 1 unassisted pull-up, learn a skate routine, write a book, create an online coaching course, do the splits, and not lose my balance and fall in Pilates class. What are things you have always wanted to learn but thought, *"I'm too old"*? List them! They can be anything big or small. Even writing the list out gives you that confidence boost. **Yes, you can do this!**

Year of Affirmation

On my blog, StylebyAngieQ, I launched a self-affirmation workshop. Each month the group chooses a new affirmation.

- **January:** Thought Affirmation
- **February:** Self-Care Affirmation
- **March:** Bedtime Affirmation
- **April:** Empowering Affirmation
- **May:** Success Affirmation
- **June:** Stress-Free Affirmation
- **July:** Growth Mindset Affirmation
- **August:** Joy Affirmation
- **September:** Letting Go Affirmation
- **October:** Confidence Affirmation
- **November:** Blessed Affirmation
- **December:** Self-Esteem Affirmation

Once I started embracing my affirmations and stopped worrying about what others thought, my evolution of me was activated. Don't hold yourself back because of self-limiting beliefs. **Activate you!** You have to strip away all the self-conscious feelings for affirmations to work. This is about you. You are worth it! Your mind is powerful, what you feed it is in your control.

Affirmations take time and habit to transform your daily life. I only allow good thoughts, and you should, too. We have no time to allow processed, self-doubter thoughts! I like to call my affirmation "my daily assistant." Whenever I feel overwhelmed and stressed, I pause, reflect, and repeat my affirmation. It's the best thing ever and it's free! You do not have to sign up for a course or buy a product. You have the power to stop a negative thought from replaying in your mind. All you have to do is **take action!**

Affirmations are attainable for everyone. You have greatness inside of you, all you have to do is believe it. No one else can do that for you.

66 Everything I need is within me.
I can do this! 99

Declare Your Affirmations

When writing this book I had one of those ah-ha! moments. I realized affirmations are in every section of my life and this book. They have become a part of who I am and how I live my life.

Time travel with me back to 1987. I was 9 years old, living my best life in neon biker shorts, creating dances to Madonna's *Like a Prayer*, and wearing the best punk rocker earrings. I was raised by a single mother who sparked my love of positive quotes. I can say she was ahead of her time, a pioneer of a positive mindset. I vividly remember one night waking up to some weird talking and realized it was coming from under my bed. (No, this is not a scary book moment!) I peeked under the bed and saw a cassette player—placed by mom—playing a Dale Carnegie course. It's safe to say affirmations and positivity are part of my DNA.

Fast forward to December 2020. I had this idea that would not leave me alone. "Create an affirmation group." I pushed it away. Tried to ignore it. It would not leave me alone. God kept putting affirmations on my heart. My response: "Lord, I have so much on my plate, I can't." And then I had a moment while getting ready one day. He showed me that this was for others—not me—and I went full force with the group.

1 Write Out Your Affirmation

My past does not define me.

Grab a notecard, piece of paper, back of a Cheez-It box—anything!—and write out your "thought affirmation." My beginning affirmation is "My thoughts do not control me. I control my thoughts and today my thoughts will be: **happy, free,** and **positive.**"

I suggest writing it out 2 times. You want your affirmation in the 2 places you spend most of your time. For me it's my desk and my bathroom mirror. (I know this makes me sound like I look at myself all day, but I swear I don't. It takes me about an hour to get ready daily, so this is where my second note card lands.) Think of the 2 places you would post your affirmation.

2 Say Your Affirmation 3 Times a Day

Say it when you wake up in the morning. Say it in the afternoon when you need that pick-me-up. And say it again before you go to bed. Repetition reinforces the message in your mind.

3 Say Your Affirmation Out Loud

The stats show that when you say your affirmation out loud, that affirmation is 10 times more powerful than the one you say in your head. **Wow!**

GIVE IT TIME

Affirmations need time and consistency to work! You are training your brain to **think positively** and push out those bad habits of negative talk.

When you break it down to basics, affirmations are all about positivity and good vibes. Over time with practice, repetition reroutes your negative thought patterns. I think about affirmations like picking up the phone and calling for a clean-up crew. Affirmations are the clean-up crew that come in with a hose and flush out all those negative thoughts.

Following the month-by-month schedule from my blog, you start off with thought affirmations, because they are crazy powerful. You are going to start off simple. You want this to become a daily habit, and if it's easy, simple, and doable, it will fit into your daily schedule.

IMPLEMENT AFFIRMATIONS THROUGHOUT YOUR DAY

In order for your affirmations to take root, sprinkle them throughout your day. **Repetition** and **consistency** are your friends!

Each day, my morning affirmation starts at the coffee pot. (You know, where all the cool kids hang out first thing.) I say that affirmation all groggily as I impatiently wait for my coffee to brew. I set an alarm in my phone to go off at 3:00 pm for my mid-day affirmation (around the same time I take that mid-day pick-me-up). This stinker—uh, I mean mid-day affirmation—kept getting away from me. I would start my day off strong and then forget by afternoon. Scheduling an alarm sets me up for success.

Without even realizing, you will be leading by example. Your kids, spouse, roommates, etc. will see these affirmations all over the house. One afternoon I was stressing. I needed to make a call to a potential client on a big account. I was nervous. I was walking around the kitchen repeating my affirmation out loud. My daughter walked around the corner and heard me and said, "That's right mom, you are a bad B!" Affirmations set the tone for positive life strategies. I'd rather my daughter hear me say affirmations out loud rather than hear me talking negatively about myself.

TRUST YOUR INSTINCTS

I run on coffee, music, and instincts. If affirmations are the first part of finding your beat, then instincts are the second part of your confidence driver. If you are not confident in the decisions you make, how can you be confident with yourself as a person? Instincts guide you. It's the part of you that is assessing the situation and sending all your feelers a message. (*Feelers*—I'm very scientific.)

Decision making is tough. If you are not careful, you can cross the line of confidence to self-doubting. No one wants to live in the self-doubter territory: overthinking, negative self-talk, doubt, and fear. Have you ever hung out with someone who lives in this territory? It's uncomfortable. All I want to do is shake them and say, "You are amazing! Knock it off!" Observing this is a nice self-check moment. When you are in tune with who you are, you're more confident in your decision making. Ask yourself, "How do I react in situations where I need to make a decision?"

"Be brave like your dreams. Dreams don't second guess. They don't doubt. They just dream!"

Mood Mover Tip!

When you have a big or small decision to make, use these strategies:

- Do not dilly dally. What was your first instinct? It's usually the one that's right for you.
- Take action.
- Take Action!
- **TAKE ACTION!**

All too often, feeling stressed about making a decision paralyzes you; avoidance replaces action and then nothing gets accomplished. Action, no matter how small, is better than doing nothing.

SMILE

Have you ever noticed how a smile from a stranger can make a huge difference in how you feel? If 2020 taught us anything it was this: **We need human interaction.** This is not a topic up for debate or discussion. A simple smile has a domino effect. It is contagious. If someone smiles at you, you naturally smile back. The benefits definitely boost your mood, give you the feel good moments in your day. Smiling reduces stress, reduces blood pressure, helps you live longer, and strengthens your immune system.

Here is the big one: **Smiling helps you stay positive!** It is free and it adds value to your life and others' lives around you!

When my kids were younger I used to tell them before they got out of the car for school, "Smile at 8 different kids today." Can you picture the rolling of the eyes? Well, it made me feel better to give them this mama advice regardless of whether they did it or not. I wanted them to share their light with others.

> **❝Be a light for all to see. ❞**
>
> —Matthew 5:16

SEEK HUMAN INTERACTION

A smile is the first step in interacting with others; it's a universal ice breaker. I have 2 teenagers: a 16-year-old and 13-year-old. My daughter will walk away from me in the grocery store the moment she feels like I am going to approach a stranger and start talking. I tell her all the time, **"It's my purpose to interact."** I need it and I'm sure this stranger needs it.

Especially after the isolation of 2020, people crave interaction. We are not designed to walk around, heads down looking at our cell phones, and only interacting in the social media world. We need real-life, feel-good interactions.

For the Love of Beet!

I recently fell in love with beets in my salad. Where have they been all my life? Beets are amazing. I was at the grocery store and decide I need beets for my salad. The problem is... well, I don't exactly know what a beet looks like. I go to the area in the produce section where I think beets would be. I'm searching, reading all the labels, and still I cannot find beets! I do one last lap around the produce section and pick up what I think might be a beet.

As I'm looking around with this might-be-a-beet in my hand, my daughter high-tails her way out of the produce section. Because, as you may have guessed, I am about to seek human interaction. I spy a nice lady who appears to be knowledgeable in cooking (and probably life) and head on over.

Me: "Excuse me, can you help me please? Is this a beet?"

Nice Lady (smiling): "Oh yes, that's a beet."

Me: "I've made at least 5 laps around this produce area waiting for someone like you to help! Thanks!"

I find my daughter and we get in line and start chatting up the cashier. See, I now have the beet but don't know how to cook it or prepare it!

Me: "Have you ever cooked a beet?

Cashier: "You know, I just love them but I've never actually cooked one!"

Me: "Well, I'm totally googling this."

Cashier: "Let know next time how it goes."
The lady in line behind me looks my way, smiling. This is all I need.

Me: "Have you ever cooked a beet before?"

Nice Lady behind me (laughing): "Nope, not once!"

In this whole shopping experience, I interacted with 3 different humans (4 if you count my embarrassed daughter). We had a light-hearted exchange, I smiled with my eyes behind my mask, and they did the same. I left Safeway feeling fulfilled. It was bigger than a beet; it was making a small difference in someone else's life.

My point is this: We never know what others are going through. A smile, a conversation, an acknowledgement can be day-changing. Acknowledgement! So many people feel like they are walking around invisible. Take a moment to see them! When you are confident with who you are, starting conversations with others is easy. You are not worried about what they are going to think, nor do you feel self-conscious. When you are open to this, you will start to see you attract interacting with others.

"Interacting is essential for your soul."

Goals

Hitting Your Mark

We live in a society that runs on instant, fast, and convenient: DoorDash, in-store pick up, grocery delivery. Goals are not instant or convenient. If it is important to you, you make time for it.

Set big goals for yourself! They are attainable. Believe in yourself!

Both long- and short-term goals require a plan of action. Lip service, hoping, and wishing are not plans. Accomplishing short-term goals gives you the gas and confidence for the dog days when you ask yourself, "Is this ever going to happen?" Short-term goals give you that boost of confidence to propel you to the finish line.

KEEP YOUR EYES ON THE PRIZE

Hitting your goals doesn't just happen. You **make** it happen! And changing your old habits can get tough. At some point (or maybe many), you'll do battle between the old version and new version of yourself. The old version fights you: *"I'm fine where I am! It's comfortable and easy here!"* The new version whispers in your other ear, *"This is the way! Keep going! I promise it's worth it!"*

You won't be able to see it at the first, it's going to take your time, and you're going to be uncomfortable, but listen: **You were made for this!** It's time to level up to the person you were made to be.

Here's how to set yourself up for success when making new goals.

❝I live outside my comfort zone. My permanent zip code: grit, bravery, vulnerability, determination. This part of town ain't for the weak. ❞

1 Write down your goal.

You are 42% more likely to achieve a goal if you write it down. Place your goal where you see it daily. I have a spot in my closet where I pin up my short- and long-term goals.

Love

2 Timeblock and take action.

Schedule goal work into your weekly calendar. Action is your secret weapon! Achieving your goal requires discipline and daily work. Carving out time daily allows you to work on your goal day-by-day; with the work you put in, your confidence builds and you get closer to your goal. When it gets cry-in-your-bed-eating-Cheez-Its-hard ask yourself, *"Am I ok delaying the person I am supposed to become? Is it ok if takes me double the time to reach this goal?"*

3 Adopt a learner mindset.

Don't come up here thinking you're all big and bad. Goals don't play nice with that kind of attitude. Surrender the knowing and **embrace the learning!** No one is expected to be perfect straight out of the gate when starting any new system or strategy. You've got to begin by embracing a learner's mindset.

Tell yourself, *"Learner territory is where I want to live. It is where I grow the most! I accept that I will make mistakes. I will not worry about what others think of me."* Read that again and let it soak in. If you are worrying about what others think of you, you will never truly embrace the process. It is not about them! **It is about you.** Take every opportunity and lesson and breathe it in.

4 Kick doubt and overthinking.

If you allow these two naysayer ambassadors into your head, you won't even take that first step toward your goals and dreams. Don't allow roadblocks to get you stuck!

Let's Do This!

5 Create a goal affirmation.

Every time you feel the naysayer ambassadors creep in, say your affirmation, like *"I got this!"* or *"Everything I need is within me"* or *"Nothing's gonna stop me!"* Anytime you feel like you want to give up on your goal, repeat your affirmation.

I Got This!

6 Honor the process.

Honor where you are in the process. Eric Thomas says, "Start with what you have because what you have is plenty." I started my coaching business in my closet, on the floor. I knew I wanted to help others and the rest would fall into place. Of course I wanted my own office, an assistant, a desk, a window, all the things. The point is what you have now is plenty to start on your goal. There is a purpose for each step, and take one step at a time. If you take on too much change all at once, *you're taking on too much.* And if you fast forward or skip a step, you miss the lesson. If you wait for everything to be perfect you will never start working on your goal.

53

7 Serve others.

When I take myself out of the goal equation and focus on helping others, nothing can stop me. Being the best version of you helps you help others to do the same.

❝I did not come this far to be AVERAGE!❞

Some days you're going to need a tough-ass mantra to keep you in check. Working on your goals is not easy. Set yourself up with strategies and tools to help you when things get tough. How would you fill in the blank?

I did not come this far to be _____!

Whenever I have a big **"girl, you better work"** goal, I like to create a specific playlist. It ultimately becomes my goal anthem and I play it whenever I need a boost in the right direction.

Boss:
The Carters

Fighter:
Christina Aguilera

All I Do Is Win:
DJ Khaled

'Till I Collapse:
Eminem

Stomp:
God's Property

Glorious:
Macklemore

We Will Rock You:
Queen

We Are the Champions:
Queen

I Just Need U:
Toby Mac

Lose Yourself:
Eminem

Hallelujah:
Tori Kelly

Jefe:
T.I. featuring Meek Mill

LAUNCH YOUR SYSTEMS

I learned from a very young age that I thrive on systems. Routine and structure make my day, relationships, and goals function. They're my go-to for keeping my life on track. **Time blocking.** Style prep. Meal plans. Weekly schedule of everybody's activities and who's doing what.

Your focus will become crystal clear with time blocking. Gone are the days of being overwhelmed with your schedule. There is a place for all your tasks and they are scheduled. Because there is a home for each task, when I get to a particular task I can focus. I am not worried about what comes next, it is there on my schedule, but for this hour I am giving my full attention to doing just what I'm doing. I trust the system!

TRY TIME BLOCKING

I discovered the magic of time blocking when I was a 5th grade teacher. My day was chunked into 6 time blocks, which made everything on my to-do list manageable. In shifting from teaching to being an entrepreneur, I knew I would be the one in charge of my own "bell schedule." I needed to create breaks, work flow, **balance.** Enter time blocking!

Time blocking is the gateway to all achieving your goals and dreams. I like to look at "big-out-of-my-comfort-zone" goals and work backward. These are the long-term goals that take a year or two to accomplish. I find the further out the goal is, the easier it is to lose sight of it. Out of sight out, of mind!

Intentionally breaking your goal into month/week/day/hour chunks gets you closer to the finish line. If you figure out how many hours you need to spend weekly on your goal you can block time for it. You are 42% more likely to accomplish a goal if you **write it out.** It is proven if you schedule time to work on your goals you are more likely to follow through. Time blocking becomes your dance partner in your goal dance.

Monday	Tuesday	Wednesday	Thursday	Friday
				8–9:00
			8–10:00	
	8–11:00			
	11–12:30			9–12:00
9–1:00		9–1:30		
1–2:00				
	12:30–3:00	1:30–3:00	10–3:00	
				12–4:30
2–5:00		3–5:30		
	3–6:30		3–6:00	

❝The moment you believe you have what it takes...that is when you are unstoppable. ❞

SELF-EVALUATION

Ok, you ready? **Let's turn up the volume!** First step in time blocking is self-evaluation. Look at your day and ask yourself these questions:

- How am I using my time?
- Am I intentional with my tasks?
- What distracts me most?
- What are my time wasters? (Interruptions? Procrastination?)
- Is my time aligned with my goals?
- When do I have the most energy?
- How long does it take me to accomplish a task?
- Am I avoiding tasks?
- What time do I wake up and go to sleep? Does the amount of sleep I get impact my energy during the day?

Whew! That's a lot to deal with. Answering these questions can help you figure out when you work best and what distracts you from accomplishing your goals. Being honest with yourself does not mean beating yourself up about the choices you make. It means reflecting, finding what you can improve on, and **taking action!**

I'm not gonna lie, I knew before I answered any of these questions social media was my biggest distraction, then text messages, and finally not honoring and protecting my time.

TAKE MINI-BREAKS

I can hold my attention for about 1 hour. Anything past that, my mind goes into overload mode. When that happens, my focus is anywhere but the task at hand. I'm planning my next vacation, wondering if FedEx has dropped off my new shoes, thinking about rearranging my pantry. This means my production level is low. In a 2017 *Forbes* article, author Kevin Kruse cites a study that **people need breaks** about every 90 minutes. Our brains need this recharge session.

Listen to your mind and body to know what your max time block is. Maybe you're a 90 minute time blocker. Make note of your patterns. When does your productivity dip? When I time block, I set my tasks in 1 hour blocks, which works best for me.

I use a simple timer. Once my timer goes off, I'm prompted to take a mini-break for 10 minutes. A 10-minute mini-break works well for my mind—it's enough, but not too much. I want to stay in the zone. Your zone may look different from mine; that's perfectly okay.

Mini-breaks can consist of grabbing a water or snack, checking the mail, having a quick dance party, meditating, walking around the building, talking to someone. **The benefits are phenomenal.** You come back to your work with a fresh perspective. Your productivity will increase with these mini-breaks, and you're less likely to burnout.

PREP YOUR WEEK ON SUNDAY

I'm a prepper. I thrive on organization and systems. Prepping is part of what keeps me focused and on-point with my goals. Here's how I do it:

1 Set Your Schedule

I block time on Sundays to organize the week ahead. I've already answered the self-evaluation questions and have all the data I need:

- I'm low on energy in the afternoon
- I'm a morning person
- I need several little breaks throughout the day
- I'm distracted by—**squirrel!**—anything!

I examine my weekly schedule and time block tasks accordingly. For example, I write content for several clients. I chose Thursday and Friday mornings from 9:00 to noon to write content, including 2 mini-breaks. I am setting myself up for success. If I schedule writing for 3:00 pm, I would be too tired, procrastinate, and push it to the next day. Then I'd feel crappy that I did. Nightly, I add any new task that has popped up on my calendar to the week.

2 Plan Your Looks

I also set myself up for success by planning my looks for the week on Sunday. I pull up my planner and base my looks around my daily activities. Once I select my looks, if I have never worn the combo before, I try it on! I want to eliminate any hidden time suckers and mood killers. And you better believe an outfit that doesn't fit or looks bad is a total killjoy for me in the morning. I'm not having any of that!

I make it fun! I set the tone and the mood for this system with music, an iced coffee, and my planner. If I have Zoom meetings on Mondays, you know I'm wearing a red lip and fun topper piece. Thursdays when I write content, I'll go for a chill vibe with a bodysuit and joggers.

Once I've approved all the looks, I place them in day-by-day order in an area of my closet I call "on deck." Monday through Friday, my looks are dialed in, on deck waiting for their debut moment. See, you are probably thinking right now, **"This chick has lost her mind!"** But don't knock it unless you try it. I spent many a high-school morning throwing a fit because I claimed I had nothing to wear. It would look like a bomb went off in my room. (Side note: I officially apologize to all the friends who I made late for school because of this.) That girl has not disappeared. Not having your look chosen can waste your time, mess with your energy, and ruin your morning.

My sister was my biggest fighter on this. I'm not exaggerating, I spent years trying to get her to buy into outfit prep. She's a boss in the corporate world with no time to waste, yet that's what she was doing every single morning. She's now a firm believer in Sunday night outfit prep. She tells me, "I am getting so many compliments on my outfits! People keep asking me if what I am wearing is new. I tell them, 'Nope. I'm shopping in my closet.'"

On a side-note, planning your weekly looks will also help you to edit your closet (see Channel Your Confidence through Style). If it never makes the weekly rotation, it's not you anymore.

3 Morning Moment

Getting ready in the morning should be a positive experience. You are **hyping yourself up** for the day! When you walk out of your house, it's your slow-mo movie moment. Pick the song, it's your moment, confidence on fire!

Take a moment and think about your mornings. What do they look like? Are you feeling the best in the look you chose? Is it thought out? Is your attitude on point or in the dumps? Set the mood for your day in the best possible way.

4 Night Time Routine

Before you go to bed, check for any mini-bombs that can go off in the morning. This also works well if you have kids. (It is never too early to teach your kids. My kids know they need to choose their clothes the night before.)

Part of my night time checklist is anything I can get out of the way that will serve me well in the morning.

- Pack lunches
- Review the look that you picked out Sunday evening
- Check your schedule for the next day
- Prep coffee so it's ready to brew (very important if you've ever run out of coffee on a Monday morning)
- Pick an affirmation to power your day

Q the Music

What can I say? **I freakin' love Mondays!** I am Monday's #1 fan! For reals I am! Sunday the anticipation starts to build— the possibility of what I can accomplish during the week. There are 52 Mondays in a year. Do not waste a single one complaining.

Naturally, I have a playlist for Monday morning:

True Reflections:
Dave Matthews Band (live version)

Walking on Sunshine:
Katrina and the Waves

Truth Hurts:
Lizzo

Keep Ya Head Up:
Tupac

Not Afraid:
Eminem

Spill the Wine:
Eric Burdon

Golden:
Harry Styles

Get Lucky:
Daft Punk (featuring Pharrel)

All Star:
Smash Mouth

Break My Stride:
Matthew Wilder

ORGANIZE BY COLOR

I color coordinate each task in my calendar. This makes me happy and I'm a firm believer if it makes you happy, do more of it! Color-coordinated planning helps you organize tasks—work, family, personal goals—however you best prioritize your time.

Last November, I made the big switch from a paper planner to a digital calendar. I was a hot mess for two weeks, but refused to give up. (I kept my paper planner next to my laptop as a security blanket, just in case I changed my mind.) It's all about your preference. Time blocking works well with both systems.

SET A TIMER

A timer and time blocking are besties! Let's go back to my #1 distraction: social media. I love it, but it is my biggest time leech. For real, no one can only spend 5 minutes on Tik Tok. It is not designed that way; it is the casino of social media—no windows, no sense of time, and all about fun and entertainment. As a social media coach, I am online often. To prevent myself from wasting time, I set a timer on my phone. I get online twice a day to engage with clients and my followers. When the timer goes off, I close the app and move on to the next thing on my schedule. It's been a game changer! Timing a particular task frees up so much time in your day. Do I time every task? No. Half of the tasks on my calendar I use a timer. Can you think of 3 tasks on your daily schedule where you could set a timer?

Timing mini-breaks is important too! As parents, entrepreneurs, busy people—especially during the pandemic when many of us were working from home—we learned the slippery slope leads from our desks to the kitchen. (Remember the children's book *If You Give a Mouse a Cookie?* This is *If You Give a Parent a Mini-break*.) You take a quick snack break. On the way to the kitchen, you notice the laundry so you pop it into the wash. Smelling the bleach wafting from the laundry, you remember you need to make a doctor's appointment. As you go to grab your phone, you walk to the kitchen and remember you were going to grab a snack. When you go to grab veggies from the fridge, you spill the contents of your lunch container and now have to clean it up. You probably see where this is going. Before you know it your 10 minute snack break has turned into an hour and 45 minutes of distractions.

Stop. Breathe. Set your timer. Those things will be there when your work day is over. You owe it to yourself to respect your time.

USE AIRPLANE MODE

"Flight 747, at this time we ask you to turn your phones to airplane mode."

Airplane mode is revolutionary for avoiding interruptions. Notifications, email pings, and text notifications are taunting distractions. They are constantly in your face, begging you to check them. Turning your phone on airplane mode during certain parts of the day saves time and distraction. Believe me, if your family needs to reach you, they will hunt you down. One hour on airplane mode is not the end of the world.

I use this all the time when I write content. Writing content for clients when I'm distracted doubles the time it takes me to complete that task. It stops the flow of my rhythm. I need momentum and airplane mode helps.

ALIGN YOUR ACTIONS TO YOUR GOALS

After implementing time blocking into your schedule, you will be shocked at how much extra time you have. Whenever I speak on this subject I get a lot of push back: "I'm a go-with-the-flow kind of person." "I don't like to be confined to a schedule." "It doesn't work in my lifestyle." The greats, the GOATS—the Greatest Of All Times!—the legends…do you think they only worked when they felt like it?

It boils down to this: it's not going to happen if you never work on it. **If it is important to you, you will make time for it.** To hit your goals, you need to align your actions to your priorities, and schedule accordingly.

RESPECT AND HONOR YOUR TIME

If you don't respect and honor your time, nobody else will, either. It's the Disney Fast Pass to your goals. I prefer not to take a detour to my goal. Schedule your goals like they are your next hair appointment. I don't know about you, but I always schedule my next hair appointment before I walk out of the salon. I never cancel my appointment unless it's a major emergency. I can't walk around with gray thinking, "Oh, I'll get to it when I get to it."

It's the same thing with goals. Moving your goal work to another time, another day, and never truly getting to it is saying, "I am ok with canceling my goals." Honor your time!

Q the Music

Your daily dose of inspo is one playlist away. I love listening to song lyrics for inspiration! I have a morning schedule of what I listen to while I get ready. I rotate: one day I listen to inspirational speeches and the next day I listen to music. Wasting time is not something I like to do, so anytime I can fit inspiration into my routine I do. Before I hop in the shower, I tell Alexa, **"Play mama the good stuff!"** Bath robe on, hair brush in hand...you better believe a concert is about to go down.

Flashdance...What a Feeling:
Irene Cara

Ain't No Mountain High Enough:
Marvin Gaye & Tammi Terrell

High Hopes:
Panic at the Disco

This Is Me:
Keala Settle & Greatest Showman Ever

Step by Step:
Whitney Houston

Life Is a Highway:
Rascal Flatts

Don't Stop Me Now:
Queen

Started from the Bottom:
Drake

Dream On:
Aerosmith

One Headlight:
Wallflowers

Good Morning:
Mandesa featuring TobyMac

WE DID IT!

I hope this book has helped you embrace your inner goal-hitting, signature-style wearing, life-living, system-loving, self-confident, I-can-do-big-things self!

Adapting these tips and tricks to fit your life can help you conquer every challenge that comes your way so you can live your life with confidence and energy. Remember to stick with it because you're worth it! **Believe in yourself** because you are an amazing, energetic, and life-loving human being who deserves every wonderful thing life has to offer.

Adapting new systems can be intimidating, but don't let fear stop you! Transformation happens when your will to change is louder than what the naysayer ambassadors say. I truly believe that this level of confidence is attainable for everyone! Once you tap into it, it is life changing! Go do your thing! Collect life, one memory at a time! You've got this!

One final thought. I believe it is only fitting to quote one of my all-time favorite movies, *Home Alone*. I leave you with the words of the infamous Kevin McCallister, "I'm not afraid anymore! Do you hear me? **I'M NOT AFRAID ANYMORE!**"

SHOUT OUTS!

To the beat that flows through my veins, my family. Start with the OG's: my Gram and Grandpa who instilled in me a crazy work ethic. A way of "you work hard, and give it your all" that way of life pushed me through completing this book when I wanted to give up—But nah…their beat pushed me along the way. To my mom, a living proof and example that NOTHING is impossible. You paved a path of independence and strength, I was watching! Thank you for igniting my love for quotes from a young age. Who would have known our refrigerator quotes from the 90's would inspire me to write the collection of affirmations. Ahhhhhh but yes, your beat pushed me through. To my dad, thank you for passing down the "grit." The grit, hustle, and classic rock helped me in my low moments. Yes, your beat was blaring loud when I wanted to just say F it!

To Sammie and Jace, you inspire me to break barriers!! Jace, thank you for reminding me to visualize my goals. Your JOYFUL beat was a constant reminder to enjoy every moment of this process! Sammie, my girl, my person! From the moment I said, "I'm going to write a book," you hyped me up. Little did you know that you inspired me to write the section "Finding Your Beat." Never forget your BEAT is special! To my sister, my Carol, my ride or die, my forever bestie. Our beat is one of the same that does not need any explanation. Your matter of fact talks gave me exactly what I needed on this journey. To my lifer, my husband. Gene, thank you for the late night walks, listening to me ramble on and on about little details in this book. You are my constant supporter in life. None of this would ever be possible without you! Your belief and support is EXTRA-ORDINARY!! It is safe to say your STRONG beat always reminded me to put 100% Angie in this book!

Thank you to the AMAZING team! I am forever grateful for your guidance. Anne, Brenda, Phyllis, you took me in with open arms and we created something life changing!!! Every step of the way all of your expertise kept me calm in this process. One word to describe this team's beat and that is CONFIDENCE.

Biggest thank you to my coach...ANNE BRUCE! When I got the text that you wanted to talk to me about something, I never in a million years expected you to say, "it's time to write a book." I thought, "she has really lost her mind." You push me to stay in learner territory and for that I thank you. Your beat was always saying, "Angie this is the way!"

My ultimate guide will always be God. I go where He leads me with the beat and talents He has instilled in me!

ABOUT THE AUTHOR

Entrepreneur, keynote speaker and coach, and roller skating enthusiast Angie Quitasol has been inspiring others since she was little. It's probably in her DNA, considering her mom used to secretly place Dale Carnegie recordings in her room as she slept.

Angie loves to help others live a life without limits. In a past life, she was an educator for 12 years, inspiring young minds as their energetic and stylish 5th grade teacher. Her natural love of style morphed into the role of fashion stylist, where she helped women find their groove and self-confidence through their own personal style.

Today, Angie is a professional speaker and social media producer and coach, motivating businesses, schools, and other entrepreneurs to increase their performance, profits, and possibilities.

Aficionado of Mondays, a good cup of coffee, a kick-butt workout, and a sassy outfit, Angie lives in Northern California with her husband, two children, and killer pink heels.

Follow her on social media at StyleByAngieQ or online at StyleByAngieQ.com.

Reinvent Your Events
with Angie Q!

Your next corporate event, team meeting, workshop, or retreat not only deserves an **energetic, fun, and dynamic presenter**—it also deserves a professional life stylist. Angie Quitasol will make sure your organization hits its target every time with the right attitude, style, confidence, and goals.

Multiple Options for All Events

Book Angie Q for your next **in-person, virtual, or hybrid event** and start finding the beat that energizes your brand and everyone on your team!

Angie's **relatable, relevant, and real world tools** can be customized to fit your organization. Angie's life-hacks and systems drive **performance, productivity, profitability, and employee engagement.**

Keynote Speech

Let's Do This! is the speech that will blow you away because it's the bomb! Takeaways include:

- time blocking system
- goal setting strategies
- digital and social media branding

Workshops and retreats based on Angie's keynote address are customized and offered in half-day and full-day sessions to help your team and business capitalize on all their possibilities.

Hire Angie to Be Your Social Media Producer

Staying connected is vital to your business' sustainability. Book Angie to teach you how to make the most of your social media presence when you:

- need a social media makeover
- are reinventing your brand and signature look
- need help in creating a social media presence that will boost business
- need to increase your influencer status

Angie's highly produced social media coaching programs include:

- one-on-one coaching sessions
- customized and e-learning courses
- executive and leadership social media branding
- social media management

Book Angie Today

For Angie's availability and fees for your next event, coaching program, or workshop call, text, or email her talent manager at (214) 507-8242 or Anne@AnneBruce.com.

Angie Quitasol

Let's Do This!

Yes! I'm interested in bringing *the Angie Q vibe* into my organization!

- Keynote Speaker

- Angie's Training Workshop

- Speak at our Retreat

- One-on-One Coaching for Leadership and Teams

- Something Super Special and Customized Just for Us!

For Angie's availability & fees, call, text, or email her talent manager at (214) 507-8242 or Anne@AnneBruce.com

Please reference Angie Q in subject line

StyleByAngieQ.com